You Gonna Touch That?

Disgusting Facts About Bugs

By Jerome Goddard, Ph.D.

Illustrated by Karen Boatman

To Emma Kate and Millie Goddard, eager listeners to Nana's "Johnny" stories.

To order additional copies of this book, contact:
Xlibris
1-888-795-4274
www.Xlibris.com
Orders@Xlibris.com

Acknowledgements

Kathy Levinson and Erica Orloff first prompted me to write this book. I'm grateful for their encouragement. Six figures in this book are from the public domain but colored by Karen Boatman. Two line drawings (kissing bug and hard tick) were originally published in a public domain Mississippi Department of Health publication called the "Mosquito Book" written and illustrated by Ed Bowles. The cockroach and army ant line drawings came from the U.S. Department of Agriculture (USDA), Agricultural Research Service (ARS), Agriculture Handbook Number 655. The mosquito drawing was published in the USDA, ARS, Agriculture Handbook Number 182, and the maggot line drawing came from the USDA Miscellaneous Publication Number 631. Publication of this book was made possible by an unrestricted educational grant from Oldham Chemicals Company, Memphis Tennessee. I am especially grateful to Tommy Reeves for their support.

TABLE OF CONTENTS

INTRODUCTION

Have you ever seen a cockroach and gotten the creeps? Or ever wondered what good mosquitoes and ticks are? You're not alone; lots of people think like that. Insects and related organisms--some people just call them all "bugs"--are everywhere. There are more of them than all other land animals. In fact, more species of insects exist than any other animal group. Insects and their kin, such as spiders, mites, ticks, and scorpions, are all placed together in one large group called "arthropods." People see arthropods all the time--sometimes inside the house, or in the office where they work, but especially outside in the yard and garden. Some of us freak out and try to chase them down and kill them. But most bugs are harmless. They are an important part of the food chain, providing food for birds and other animals. Plus, bees are needed for pollinating flowers and fruits. Some bugs have disgusting habits--like eating poop, or squirting out stinky juices, or drinking blood. And there are some harmful bugs--ones that can sting, bite, or even transmit disease germs. Perhaps more than anybody, kids almost constantly encounter bugs. Therefore, it's a good idea to know something about them--which ones are harmful, which ones are weird, and which ones are just plain disgusting.

Chapter One

Beetles That Like Poop

A lot of people don't know it, but beetles (like butterflies) have four life stages--egg, larva, pupa, and adult. The beetle larva is a worm-like creature which feeds on roots of plants, decaying logs, or other stuff like that. One group of beetles--the scarab beetles--includes the "dung" beetles. They are named that because the larvae eat animal poop! They like it. It's all juicy and stuff, and full of protein and other nutrients. These beetles either tunnel under a big pile of poop and lay their eggs (so the babies don't have to go far for food), or make a tunnel and put poop inside it for the babies. Actually, dung beetles do a good thing for the environment by getting rid of animal poop. They are like nature's housekeepers.

Gross Examples: Some dung beetle species roll up a huge ball of moist, stinky animal poop and then bury it in an underground chamber. Sometimes you can see these beetles on the ground wrestling around with a big ball, trying to get it moved to the chamber. The dung ball is usually much bigger than the beetle, and they move it by walking backward and pushing it.

The female lays an egg on or in the dung ball (some scientists call this an "egg ball"). The ball of poop serves as food for the new babies when they hatch.

Certain species of dung beetles in India make the egg balls huge and coat them with clay. They can be as big as a soft ball. When these big things were first discovered, archeologists thought they were ancient stone cannon balls! And some of them were found 8 feet below the ground. Wonder how the bugs got those things that far down in the ground?

Weird Facts About Dung Beetles: You wouldn't think that poop-eating bugs would be pretty, but some dung beetles are extremely beautiful, being shiny metal-colored green and pink. Others have a huge horn like a rhinoceros. They don't use the big horn for making or moving the dung balls, but instead, for fighting with other dung beetles.

One species of dung beetle, called by its scientific name, *Onthophagus gazella*, can bury a patty of elephant dung in one night. Think of how much poop an elephant makes. In Africa, piles of animal poop rarely last through the night. The beetles get them. They're gone. Poof! Just like that!

The ancient Egyptians made stone images of scarab beetles to be used as religious ornaments. The sacred scarab of Egypt, *Scarabaeus sacer*, was a dung beetle. In Egyptian mythology the ball of dung represented the earth and its rotation.

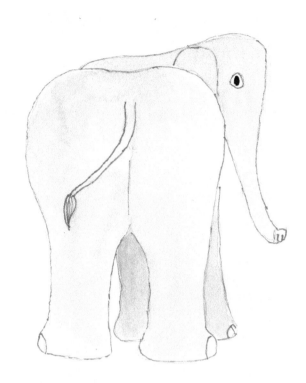

Chapter Two

Beetles That Squirt Junk On You

Bugs have all kinds of ways of protecting themselves from attack or being eaten by birds, frogs, lizards, and even other insects. Some insects can sting, bite, or use camouflage to fight off or avoid predators. But some beetles do a weird thing when attacked––they squirt out stinky junk. And it's not poop. They aren't pooping because they're scared. They are purposely squirting out a foul-smelling substance to make the attacker go away.

Gross Examples: Members of the ground beetle genus *Calosoma* are called caterpillar hunters because they catch caterpillars. They are about an inch and a half long, and are a beautiful metallic green and blue color. If you pick one up, it gives off a really foul odor, making your hands all stinky for a long time. I've had my hands stink for a week after collecting these things. No matter how many times I washed my hands.

There is another ground beetle species, *Nomius pygmaeus*, which occasionally invades homes in the western United States. It puts out stinky juice everywhere. It is so stinky that any household item where this beetle has crawled stinks for weeks!

Beetles in the genus *Eleodes*––called Darkling beetles––not only squirt out a stinky reddish black juice when disturbed or picked up, but run around wildly with their rear ends stuck almost straight up in the air. These beetles are often called, "stink beetles." And I'm not kidding when I say their juice stinks. One college textbook on entomology says, "They secrete an evil smelling defensive fluid from the anal end of the body."

Weird Facts About Ground and Darkling Beetles: Species of ground beetles in the genus *Brachinus* are bright blue and are called bombardier beetles because not only do they squirt out juices, they blow them out like a bomb! The beetle mixes some juices together inside its abdomen which explode with a loud pop. It looks like a puff of smoke coming out the beetle's back end. Boom! Just like a cannon.

The ground beetle, *Calosoma sycophanta*, a brilliant green caterpillar-hunting species, is one of the species that will stink up your hands if you pick them up. This beetle was purposely brought into the United States from Europe and released in the forests to help control the gypsy moth (a bad pest of trees). This beetle runs around on the ground gobbling up the larval gypsy moths. Yum yum, eat 'em up!

Chapter Three

FLIES THAT LIKE DEAD
OR STINKY THINGS

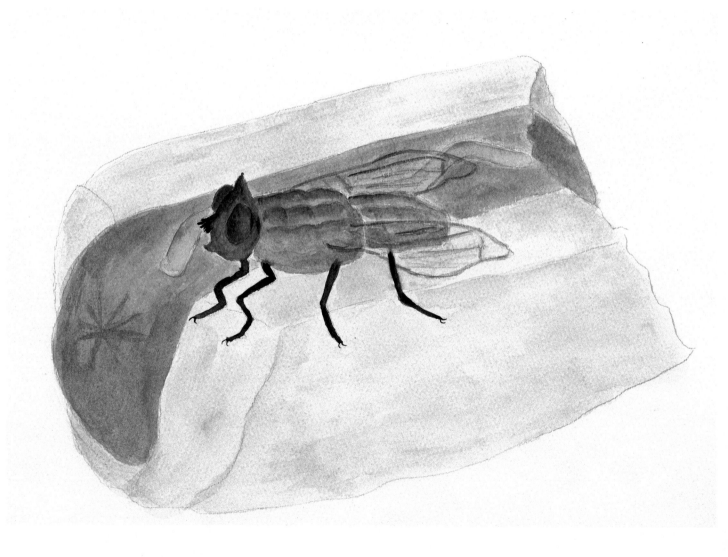

Like butterflies and beetles, flies also have a larval stage which looks like a worm and feeds on a wide variety of substances. The larva then turns into a pupa (making a structure similar to a cocoon), and later emerges as an adult fly. The adult flies will land on food--like your hot dog or sandwich--and try to eat them or lay eggs. Larval flies--called maggots-- eat decaying organic matter such as garbage, animal poop, or rotten vegetation. A long time ago, when people had to go to the bathroom outside in a thing called an outhouse, flies were always buzzing around because it was so stinky. Fly maggots belonging to the insect families Calliphoridae and Sarcophagidae are called blow flies and flesh flies. Know why? They eat dead animals! When an animal dies in the forest or gets killed on the highway, adult blow flies and flesh flies come lay eggs on the dead body. Soon the eggs hatch and thousands of little white maggots start eating the stinky, juicy carcass. This behavior is actually a good thing because it helps keep the environment clean. Think of how many dead animals would be on the road if it weren't for fly maggots.

Gross Examples: Blow flies and flesh flies come to a dead animal at different times during the rotting process. Some are attracted when it is freshly dead, while others wait until it is more swollen and rotten. Blow flies––especially species in the genus *Calliphora* and *Lucilia*––come to a dead animal almost immediately after death. We're talking 5 minutes or so. It's funny how they know the difference between a sleeping animal and a dead animal.

People used to grow their own food and cure their own meat, like ham and bacon. And blow flies were a bad problem because they would get on the food. When people would put fruit out in the sun––like sliced apples–– to dry, or hang meat in a storehouse, the blow flies would come buzzing in and lay thousands of eggs on the food. Soon, maggots were everywhere. How would you like to eat some of the food covered with maggots?

Weird Facts About Flesh and Blow Flies: One of the largest and most common flesh flies, *Sarcophaga hemorrhoidalis*, has a big red rear end. That might be why it's named "hemorrhoidalis."

A female of the blow fly, *Cochliomyia macellaria*, can lay up to 1,000 or more eggs on a dead animal in groups of 40-250 eggs each.

Blow flies and flesh flies come to dead people as well––like at a murder scene. And scientists can use information about the maggots to determine how long the person has been dead.

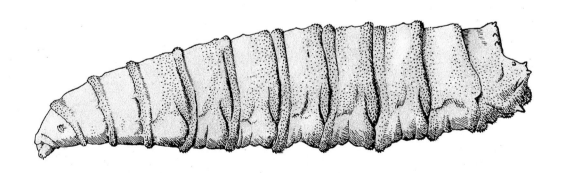

Scientists who do this kind of thing are called "forensic entomologists." This is how it works. When somebody is found murdered out in the woods or somewhere like that, the police investigators collect all kinds of evidence at the place. One thing they do is to collect fly maggots. Blow fly species come to a dead person within five minutes or so after being killed or placed outside. The bug person knows what the weather has been like at the place where the body was found (you can get this information from the National Weather Service). The entomologist then looks through the crime scene evidence for maggots *of that species* (the ones that come first). He or she examines the maggots to see what stage they are in--like first, second, or third stage maggot.

Then, the bug person calculates how long it would take for that maggot to develop to that stage under those weather conditions. And that's how long the dead person has been out there in the woods!

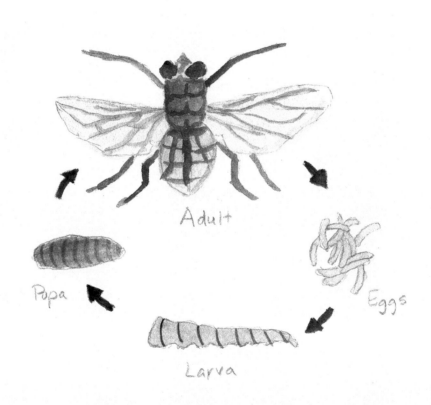

Adult

Eggs

Larva

Pupa

Chapter Four

TICKS THAT SWELL
UP WITH BLOOD

Ticks are some of the grossest bugs on earth (even though they really are not insects, but instead, arachnids). They have eight legs and (what appears to be) one egg-shaped body region. They don't actually have a head, but do have mouthparts which stick out front. Although they may be important in the "web of life," ticks seem to serve no useful purpose in the world except to get on animals or people and suck blood. Because of their lifestyle, they are considered parasites––living off of another living thing without giving any benefit to the other organism. Both male and female ticks attach to animals or people and suck blood, but the female tick swells up with blood until she's HUGE! She starts out flat and about the size of your little fingernail, but drinks blood until she's about the size of a big fat grape. Then she lets go, falls to the ground, crawls under a leaf or stone, and lays eggs to start the life cycle over again.

Ticks have medical importance as well. There are several real bad human diseases carried by ticks, such as Lyme disease, Rocky Mountain spotted fever, relapsing fever, and others. When a tick sucks your blood, it may transmit the disease germ to you. That doesn't mean that every tick has a disease germ in it, but some of them do. It's like a needle in a haystack—only one out of every-so-many hundred or thousand have disease germs in them.

Gross Examples: The lone star tick, *Amblyomma americanum*, is a very common tick in much of the eastern United States. Both the male and female are reddish brown, but the female has  a single white dot on her back and the male has several white squiggly marks on his back. This tick is fast and mean. It can get on you (while you are outside walking in the weeds) and crawl up to your head in about one minute. All stages of this tick––adults and babies––will eagerly bite people. The female, after swelling up with blood, can lay up to 8,000 eggs. How would you like to sit down where those eggs have just hatched?

The brown dog tick, *Rhipicephalus sanguineus*, is a real bad pest of dogs. Both the male and female are small, brownish colored ticks with no white markings on them. They wait in the grass and then get on pet dogs, especially in the ears.

I have seen dogs with over a thousand brown dog ticks in one ear! And, homes with pet dogs can become severely infested with thousands of this tick crawling around on the walls and furniture.

Weird Facts About Ticks: Some tick species can make a person paralyzed. While the tick is attached and sucking blood, the victim soon gets unable to  walk or stand. Scientists think the paralysis is caused by certain substances in the tick spit (saliva) which are injected while sucking blood. The good thing is that the patient starts getting better almost instantly after the tick is found and removed.

Some ticks bite almost any animal, but others are extremely picky in what they will bite. In other words, they ONLY want to bite certain animals. There is a rabbit tick, *Haemaphysalis leporispalustris*, which is on rabbits out in the woods. But that tick species won't bite you even if you let a hundred of them crawl all over you! Because you're not a rabbit.

Chapter Five

CATERPILLARS THAT STING

Caterpillars are the larval stage of butterflies and moths and can be found outdoors eating leaves of various plants or trees. Most kids have at one time or another caught one in a jar, kept it until it made a cocoon, and later watched it emerge as a beautiful butterfly or moth. You can pick up and play with most caterpillars, but a few of them can sting and should not be touched. The stinging caterpillars may even look pretty with red dots or green patterns on their back, but they have poisonous hairs or spines on them which poke into your skin and squirt out a little venom. This venom––just like that found in a wasp stinger––causes pain, swelling, and itching.

People can become allergic to stinging caterpillars just like they do to any other stinging insect. In that case, the person after being stung may swell up, get a rash all over the body, have difficulty breathing, and maybe die. Fortunately, very few people actually die from sting allergies. Also, there's a medicine for allergic reactions to stings which can save your life if used right away.

Gross Examples: The saddleback caterpillar, *Sibine stimulea*, is about an inch long, has a brown, slug-like body, and stout prickly spines at both ends. It is called the "saddleback" because of markings on its back which look like a brown or purple saddle placed on a green and white saddle blanket.

The puss caterpillar doesn't even look like a caterpillar. It looks more like a little patch of tan fur or cotton. It doesn't have hard spines, but the hairs contain venom which causes severe pain in people. One woman stepped on a puss caterpillar and almost instantly had a burning pain in her foot. Within minutes, she was having shooting pains in her leg and a hard time breathing. She was having an allergic reaction (like described above) to the sting, and almost died!

Weird Facts About Stinging Caterpillars: Certain caterpillar stings are so painful that doctors describe it as "intense stabbing pain." The pain is rhythmic, coming and going like the beat of a drum. I don't know about you, but I don't want that!

In the 1930's the schools in San Antonio, Texas

had to be closed for days because of puss caterpillars. There were millions of the little things everywhere—bushes, fences, walls, etc. You couldn't help from brushing up against one and getting stung.

Sometimes the spines of a stinging caterpillar leave a mark on your skin shaped just like the caterpillar. It's like a tracing of the caterpillar on your skin. In that case, doctors don't have a hard time figuring out what's wrong with you. There's a drawing of the problem right there on the skin!

Chapter Six

SPIDERS THAT KILL

Like ticks, spiders are arachnids and not true insects. They have eight legs and two body regions. Lots of people are scared to death of spiders, probably because of their creepy appearance and all those legs. But spiders are actually very good in the outdoors because they catch and eat other insects, thus keeping them under control. Can you imagine how many flies there would be in the world if spiders didn't keep eat them, keeping them under control? Anyway, some spiders are dangerous to humans because their venom either makes you really sick, or makes ugly scars on your skin. Spiders have venom (and need it) because they catch things, inject venom, wait for the venom to dissolve the guts, and then suck it back up. That's the way they eat things. Problem is, venom of some species dissolves human skin, leaving a big sore! Or worse, the venom may make you ill or even kill you. Fortunately, only a very few spiders are dangerous to people.

Gross Examples: Black widow spiders are shiny black with a bright red hourglass-shaped marking on their belly. They are about the size of a nickel or a quarter (legs included) and are not hairy. Black widows can often be found outside in places like fences, in rock piles, water meters, stacks of bricks or concrete blocks. They aren't all that mean, but will bite if touched or handled. Most people who get bit by a black widow do not die, but can get very sick with symptoms such as extreme pain, nausea (feeling like you are going to throw up), weakness, and even convulsions. Fortunately, doctors have medicines to treat symptoms of black widow poisoning. I'm glad of that, aren't you?

Brown recluse spiders––often called violin or fiddle-back spiders––are about the size of a quarter (including legs) and are tan to brown. On their back is a violin-shaped figure. Brown recluses may be found outside–– like in a pile of bricks––but are often found indoors in areas of clutter, such as attics, closets, or basements. Like black widows, brown recluses are really not very mean. In fact, they are called "recluses" because they hide a lot. People usually only get bitten when putting on clothing containing hidden spiders or something like that. People who get bit by brown recluses may develop a big sore––big around as a golf ball or bigger––that is slow to heal. It may even rot out, leaving a bad scar.

Funnel web spiders live in Australia and are extremely dangerous. They are about the size of a half dollar (including legs) and are dark brown to black. Funnel web spiders have big curved fangs which they show off by rearing up on their hind legs––just like a horse. People bitten by these spiders get very sick with muscle pains, difficulty breathing, and very low blood pressure. They must get medical attention immediately. I don't know about you, but I don't want to meet up with a funnel web spider!

Weird Facts About Spiders: The Sydney funnel web spider is so venomous that it can kill a human in 15 minutes. Fortunately, there is an antivenom––a medicine which can prevent death if the person is treated quickly.

The North American tarantulas, although big and mean-looking, are not venomous. Bites by tarantulas may be painful for an hour or so, but really are not serious.

Tarantulas have irritating hairs on their abdomen which they can throw at you! These hairs are flicked off by the spiders as a defensive mechanism. Like throwing darts. If the hairs get on your skin they may cause itching for several days.

There's a large tarantula in South America which can catch birds and eat them! This spider, *Avicularia avicularia*, is huge with a leg span of about seven inches. That's as big as a pie plate in your mother's kitchen. One scientist studying the spider said that he saw some them in Venezuela running up and down trunks of trees with "astonishing rapidity." That means he couldn't believe how fast they were. Apparently, this spider is fast enough and big enough to catch and wrestle down a small bird. It then sucks the bird dry of its bodily fluids.

Chapter Seven

Cockroaches That
Love Nasty Stuff

Of all bugs on earth, cockroaches are probably the most disliked. That doesn't mean that people are more scared of cockroaches than any other bug, only that they hate them more than other bugs. People are disgusted by them, and will go to any length--even paying lots of money to exterminators--to get rid of them. Cockroaches can make you sick, but not because of biting. Roaches don't bite, although they might feebly nibble at people's skin or fingernails. They are medically important because of their nasty habits. They love stinky, nasty places like sewers, bathrooms, and storm drains. Walking around in all that sewage, vomit, poop, and other wastes gets germs on their body parts. When the roaches later crawl up on your table or even food, they may carry germs.

Gross Examples: The American cockroach, *Periplaneta americana*, lives outdoors in storm drains, sheds, alleys, and places like that. They love dog pens because of all the dog food and dog poop there. Roaches freely enter houses and restaurants looking for other sources of food and water. One time I went to a restaurant for an inspection. Guess what I saw? A huge cockroach coming up out of the floor drain and heading right toward the food on the counter!

Cockroaches give off a nauseous juice from both their mouths and certain glands, making a stinky "cockroach odor." Pest exterminators say they can tell which houses and apartments have roaches because of this smell. Exterminators don't even have to look— they can smell the roaches! Have you ever smelled cockroaches?

Weird Facts About Cockroaches: Cockroaches can live several months without water and even longer without food. They will eat almost anything, including paper, clothes, books, hair, shoes, dried blood, dead insects, poop, and even spit!

A cockroach can live for many hours without its head. They'll just walk around as if nothing's wrong! I guess they don't even need a head.

Cockroaches have been reported to eat on the fingernails or toenails of sleeping people, and even be living in the hair of people who don't take baths!

Some tropical species of cockroaches are pretty, being brilliantly colored green, blue, yellow, and even red.

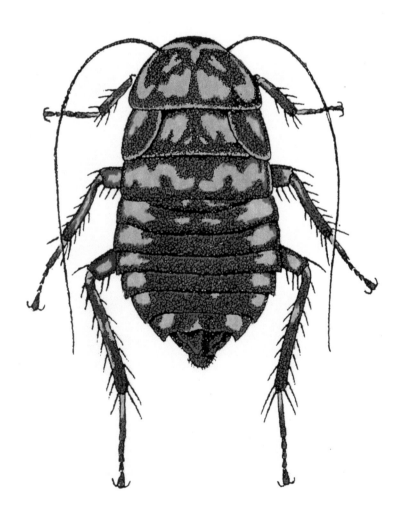

Chapter Eight

Mosquitoes That Carry Deadly Diseases

The mosquito is the deadliest animal on the earth. People don't understand this statement, but it's true. Mosquitoes—as well as all other insects—are animals (Well, they aren't plants, are they?). And mosquitoes carry one of the worst human diseases in the world—malaria. Like ticks or fleas, mosquitoes must suck blood to complete their life cycle. Since they might suck blood from a bird or rat one time, and from a human the next time, all sorts of really bad diseases can be picked up and transmitted to you by their bite.

Mosquitoes breed in water and live almost everywhere. In fact, some of the worst mosquito problems in the world are way up north—like in Alaska! At certain times of the year, there are so many of them in Alaska that you have to wear a head net to keep from breathing them in. They have adapted to almost all sources of water to lay eggs in. For example, some mosquitoes breed in swamps, some in lakes, some in old discarded tires or cans, clogged rain gutters, bird baths, tire tracks in the mud, rice fields, and so on.

Gross Examples: There are about 200 million cases of malaria in the world each year caused by mosquitoes, with about 500,000 deaths. Two hundred million is about half the population of the United States. Dengue fever, another mosquito-carried disease, is almost everywhere in the tropics. There are about 400 million cases of it each year. About 100 different viruses are transmitted by mosquitoes, including Zika and West Nile virus, and a funny one named "O'nyong nyong" Can you say that word?

Weird Facts About Mosquitoes That Carry Deadly Diseases: Dengue fever, carried by mosquitoes, is called "breakbone fever" because it feels like all your bones are breaking. Crunch, crunch, hurt, hurt!

Some mosquitoes carry tiny worms and spit them into you by biting! Most of these diseases occur in tropical countries, but one such mosquito-carried disease in the United States is dog heartworm. The tiny worms get inside the dog's heart. Fortunately, veterinarians have a medicine to prevent dog heartworm.

Adult mosquitoes live about a month. Only the female mosquito feeds on blood. She uses the blood to make her eggs.

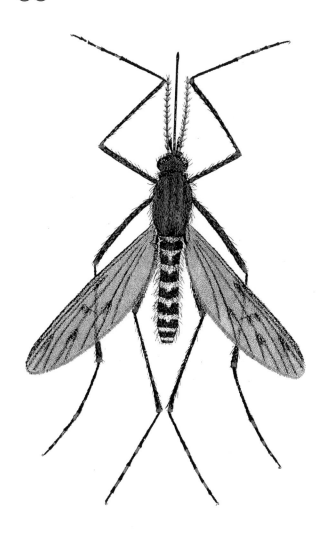

Some mosquitoes are actually very beautiful. One species, *Uranotaenia sapphirina*, has lines of brilliant blue scales on it that look just like tiny jewels glued to its back and side. Looking at one of the mosquitoes under a microscope is awesome!

Chapter Nine

Dangerous Ants That Can Take Over Land

Ants are amazing creatures. They are highly social--working together as a group for the good of the colony. Each ant knows its job in the colony and works tirelessly. Most ants are helpful to the ecosystem, but a few species are dangerous pests. Two ant groups are so successful at nest building, society organizing, and looking for food that they actually "take over" areas of land, making life miserable for humans and other animals.

Gross Examples: Imported fire ants were accidentally brought into the United States from South America in the 1930's. Ever since, they have spread throughout

the southern states all the way to California. Fire ants get their name from the fact that their sting burns like fire. They bite with their mouthparts, chomping down on your skin, then sting you with the rear end. Making things worse, they are extremely mean. If you disturb a nest (mound), the fire ants explode out of the mound stinging everything in sight. It's not unusual for a person living in fire ant infested areas to get hundreds of fire ant stings. Fire ants are very successful in making nests in new areas. Depending upon soil conditions, they build mounds on the ground. In some places these mounds are almost 3 feet high. Usually there are about 30-50 fire ant mounds on one acre of land, but some places have up to 300-400 mounds per acre. One time I went to a place in Texas where there were so many fire ants that there was no place to stand without getting stung by the ants! It made me just want to run away screaming!

Army ants are huge tropical ants which go into "nomadic" phases where they march––by the millions––into new areas catching food. Seems like they are always out looking around in hills and valleys for food. Army ants do what is called group predation, because the ant colony acts as one organism, moving along the ground catching food such as tarantulas, scorpions, beetles, roaches, grasshoppers, other ants, and even occasionally snakes and lizards. Like fire ants, army ants sting their prey. When army ants are on the move, they travel in distinct files or "armies." Some species travel along in columns, whereas others travel in fan-shaped masses. During the nomadic or "moving" phase the colony changes its nesting site every day for about three weeks. These daily shelters are called bivouacs. Then they enter a stationary phase where they stay put for 2-3 weeks while the queen lays a batch of eggs.

Weird Facts About Invasive Ants: One scientist reported a large fish kill resulting from bluegill sunfish eating fire ants.

Apparently, the ants stung the fish inside the mouth and stomach!

Although people can become allergic to fire ant stings and die from just a few stings, some people can be stung numerous times without much harm. One lady was stung by over 10,000 fire ants and lived! Oooweee!

Army ants advancing in a column travel at a speed of 30-40 meters per hour!

At night in a bivouac, army ants link their legs and bodies together with their strong claws, forming chains and nets that make layers and layers of ants, almost like a solid ball or cylinder.

In the jungle you can find a colony of raiding army ants just by listening! There are all kinds of noises associated with the moving ants--rustling of leaves as they move along the ground; small animals and insects trying to get away from the advancing army; and all kinds of flies hovering, circling, and darting over the advancing column.

One species of army ant, *Dorylus wilverthi*, has from 2-15 million members in one colony! How would you like for them to come up into your back yard?

Chapter Ten

SCORPIONS——ARACHNIDS
WITH THE POISONOUS TAIL

Scorpions are eight-legged, lobster-like arachnids. They have a stinger at the end of their tail and pincers near their head, always ready to catch and hold their prey. They walk around with the stinger raised upright and thrust forward over their back. When scorpions catch something to eat--like an insect, spider, or lizard--they paralyze it with their sting. There are about 1,400 species of scorpions occurring almost everywhere on earth, but are more numerous in dry sandy areas.

Gross Examples: Scorpion stings hurt. And some species have deadly venom--powerful enough to kill a person in a couple of hours. The really bad scorpions may make you have cramps, blurry vision, paralysis (can't move), muscle twitching, rapid heartbeat, seizure-like movements, and convulsions. In the United States there are lots of scorpion species, but only one is considered dangerous-- *Centruroides sculpturatus.* I wouldn't call it deadly, but some people have died from it. This scorpion occurs in Arizona and New Mexico, extending down into Baja California.

In Brazil, there are an estimated 5,000 scorpion stings in people each year with about 50 deaths. In North Africa, there is a scorpion––called the fat-tailed scorpion––which is responsible for 80% of all scorpion stings; about a third of the people die! This scorpion likes to get in your shoes at night. When you put them on the next morning, "Awwooo!"

There's a very common scorpion in Texas, *Centruroides vittatus*, which is not deadly, but has a sting as painful as that of a wasp or bee. It is very often found in people's bed or bathtub! One woman in south Texas told me that she has often awakened at night and seen them crawling on her ceiling right above her! Would you like to get into a bathtub with a scorpion?

Weird Facts About Scorpions: Baby scorpions are born alive (not eggs), and climb onto their mother's back where they remain for about two weeks. Can you imagine stomping one of these and the babies scattering everywhere? What if one ran up your leg?

You can't judge how poisonous a scorpion is by its size. Huge, ugly ones as big as your hand are harmless, while some little ones not much bigger than a paper clip are deadly.

There are scorpions living on snow-covered mountains over 16,000 feet high. Several species live in caves, and one species, *Alacran tartarus*, is found at depths underground of more than 2,000 feet!

Scorpions have an extremely low metabolic rate, and can survive a year or more without food. Many species spend 95% of their entire lives inside their burrows not moving. Not a very exciting life, huh?

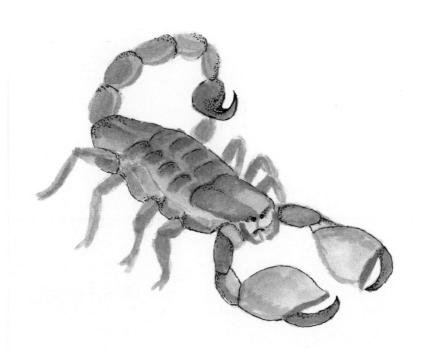

Chapter Eleven

BUGS THAT KISS YOU GOODNIGHT

There is a group of insects called "kissing bugs" because of their nasty habit of sucking blood from around your lips at night. Kissing bugs are about an inch and a half long, have a long, snout-like head, and some are marked with orange and black markings. There are at least 100 species occurring in the southern United States, down into Central and South America. The name "kissing bug" is actually wrong, because they will suck blood from other places on your body beside the lips––like your hands or feet. In nature, they live in animal nests and burrows (where they suck blood from the animals), but they will infest houses, especially primitive ones made of wood, mud, or thatch (plant material arranged in thick mats). Some kissing bugs transmit a real bad disease––called Chagas' disease––when they bite. This disease causes damage to your heart muscle. Chagas' disease is pretty common in Mexico and Central and South America. Only a few dozen cases have ever occurred in the United States.

Gross Examples: It usually takes 10-25 minutes for a kissing bug to fill up with blood. During the time they are feeding on a person, the bugs poop. The poop is a juicy, half-liquid stuff which contains the Chagas' disease germs. Later, when the person scratches his or her skin, the germs get scratched into the bite site, causing disease. So, Chagas' disease is really not spread by the bite, but by the poop!

Kissing bugs love thatch roofed huts. The bugs hide up in the thatch and wait for you to come in and go to sleep. They watch you and know when you're asleep. Then they fly down to suck blood. If you get to go to Central or South America and someone asks you to spend the night in thatched roof hut, watch out! Better keep the light on!

Weird Facts About Kissing Bugs: Some species of kissing bugs hurt when they bite, others can bite without you ever knowing it. They have adapted to make their bites totally painless, so you'll never know they've been there. Except, I guess, they might leave some poop on your skin!

Adult kissing bugs can drink 4 times their body weight in blood.

One way to tell if kissing bugs are inside a house is to look for streaks of black and white poop on the walls and furniture.

About the Author

Jerome Goddard is a bug professor at Mississippi State University in Starkville, Mississippi. He went to college for ten years to study bugs of every type, but especially ones that can hurt you. Every day at work he identifies weird bugs brought in by people, researches them, and even dissects them to study their guts! Dr. Goddard is fascinated with bugs and he hopes you will be too.

Mr. Jerome, the bug man, will be glad to answer your questions. You may contact him at jeromegoddard10@yahoo.com

Printed in the United States
By Bookmasters